THE ANNOTATED ASHTAVAKRA GITA

ANNOTATED

ASHTAVAKRA GITA

THE SONG
(ASHTAVAKRA SAMHITA)

Translated by John Richards

WWW.BIGFONTBOOKS.COM
ISBN: 978-1-957990-53-8

Contents

Preface

Who was Ashtavakra? It's a long story. Reference can be found in the Mahabharata. Asked about who he is, how he became to have that name, Ashta, in Sanskrit means eight and Vakra means crooked, curved, bent. This person was so intriguing because, according to the lore, he was born with eight deformities in his body. He had two deformed feet, two deformed knees, two deformed hands, a deformed chest and a deformed head.

And the way he got this was because when he was in the womb, his father, who was a great Vedic scholar who was in the habit of chanting the Veda. And it's very important that when you chant the Veda every syllable and every how long the syllable is held and so many of the rules. From the womb he criticized his father;

He said, Dad, you made eight mistakes. So the father was so enraged by this. He says, I curse you to have eight deformities. So he comes out, he's got these deformities, but he's a genius in the study of the Vedanta scriptures. And as the story goes, his father gets into trouble because he's defeated in the court of King Janaka. And so to rescue his father, he goes to the court to defeat another scholar in debate. And if he wins, his father gets freed and he wins the debate. In the end Janaka is so impressed that he says, I want you to teach me. So this song is the teaching. Even though Janaka is considered a highly enlightened king, he's still not fully realized.

Ashtavakra was supposed to be the realized sage, and he's going to teach King Janaka. There's a famous verse where Janaka says; Even if my whole kingdom burns. Nothing of mine is burnt. Which shows that he's very detached king and has wisdom, but he's not self realized. He's qualified for the highest teaching. We have to understand, because this is teaching from the highest point of view to the highest qualified student. The student who has the qualities that makes them qualified to study Vedanta primarily are a burning desire for liberation and a dispassionate disposition for the impermanent pleasures that we find in the world. Those are the main qualities.

Andras M. Nagy
Woodland California 2022

I Vision of the Self as the All-pervading Witness

Janaka:

1 How is knowledge to be acquired? How is liberation to be attained? And how is dispassion to be reached? Tell me this, sir.[1]

---

1   Vedic teaching is not merely for intellectual satisfaction nor a wonderful curiosity of how different people saw things, but the whole purpose was that I want to put an end to all my suffering, all my fears, all my desires is bothering me, and I want to be infinitely happy, unending happiness, the end of suffering and the attainment of endless bliss. That's called Mukti. So philosophy was not really for the purpose of philosophy, but that by doing this type of inquiry. Self inquiry one could attain. Mukti So Janika says, How will I attain Mukti? Because that's what he wants. He's heard that in the Upanishads. It says Brahma viewed from above into the knower, the absolute becomes the absolute bliss.

Ashtavakra:

2 If you are seeking liberation, my son, shun the objects of the senses like poison. Practise tolerance, sincerity, compassion, contentment and truthfulness like nectar.

3 You are neither earth, water, fire, air or even ether. For liberation know yourself as consisting of consciousness, the witness of these.

4 If only you will remain resting in consciousness, seeing yourself as distinct from the body, then even now you will become happy, peaceful and free from bonds.

5 You do not belong to the Brahmin or any other caste, you are not at any stage, nor are you anything that the eye can see. You are unattached and formless, the witness of everything - so be happy.

6 Righteousness and unrighteousness, pleasure and pain are purely of the mind and are no concern of yours. You are neither the doer nor the reaper of the consequences, so you are always free.

7 You are the one witness of everything, and are always totally free. The cause of your bondage is that you see the witness as something other than this.

8 Since you have been bitten by the black snake of the self- opinion that 'I am the doer', drink the nectar of faith in the fact that 'I am not the doer', and be happy.

9 Burn down the forest of ignorance with the fire of the understanding that 'I am the one pure awareness', and be happy and free from distress.

10 That in which all this appears - imagined like the snake in a rope, that joy, supreme joy and awareness is what you are, so be happy.

11 If one thinks of oneself as free, one is free, and if one thinks of oneself as bound, one is bound. Here this saying is true, "Thinking makes it so".[2]

2   *Merely imagining that you are free will take you nowhere. You have to see the truth of it and know that you are free. So that's how I interpreted the verse. The self is the witness. All pervading, Perfect One. Pure consciousness. Without any action. It appears as if it is*

12 Your real nature is as the one perfect, free, and actionless consciousness, the all-pervading witness - unattached to anything, desireless and at peace. It is from illusion that you seem to be involved in Samsara.[3]

13 Meditate on yourself as motionless awareness, free from any dualism, giving up the mistaken idea that you are just a derivative consciousness, or anything external or internal.

14 You have long been trapped in the snare of identification with the body. Sever it with the knife of knowledge that 'I am awareness', and be happy, my son.

15 You are really unbound and actionless, self-illuminating and spotless already. The cause of your bondage is that you are still resorting to stilling the mind.

---

the world. Through illusion. Even though the self is always the witness, that's its unchanging nature. It's never the witness which is the world.
3   Samsara that means "world". It is also the concept of rebirth and "cyclicality of all life, matter, existence"

16 All of this is really filled by you and strung out in you, for what you consist of is pure awareness - so don't be small minded.

17 You are unconditioned and changeless, formless and immovable, unfathomable awareness and unperturbable, so hold to nothing but consciousness.[4]

18 Recognise that the apparent is unreal, while the unmanifest is abiding. Through this initiation into truth you will escape falling into unreality again.

---

4   *When we see the absolute point of view. What we really mean is that from the absolute point of view, there's just one reality. Without a second. That's called Advaita. No duality. There's just one reality. In that reality. There's nobody in bondage. Nobody needs to be liberated, there are no gurus. There's no teaching will be done there. There's no time. There's no space, there's no creation, there's no destruction. There's nobody caught up in birth and death. All of that is not the absolute point of view will be that. And all the teaching about you don't know the self because of your ignorance, your suffering, and. When you get rid of that ignorance, you'll be free.*

19 Just as a mirror exists everywhere both within and apart from its reflected images, so the Supreme Lord exists everywhere within and apart from this body.[5]

---

5   *It's the eternal subject which can never be objectified, which doesn't have to be objectified because you can intuit it. As your true nature without objectively. You have been bitten by the great black serpent, a false notion of I am the doer. Please drink the nectar of the belief. I am not a doer it and be happy. This idea that I'm the doer, in control. That I think that I'm doing so. That I'm thinking that I'm. See that I'm talking. I'm the doer. This very root belief that we all have. I'm the agent. I lifted my leg. I put it down. That's what I did. This belief that I am the doer. So we should drink the nectar of liberation. Of the intuition, which was unwritten. The belief be in the nectarine belief. That I am not the doer. How do you get that intuition? By directly recognizing a fact that I'm the witness and I don't do anything. By that recognition. The idea I am the doer, which is the black serpent that is dissolved. All of us will be put to an end. That nectar puts an end to the poison. It's the medicine that's required. Having thus burned down the forest of ignorance. Because of this ignorance, it becomes the forest of Samsara. Once again, this body,*

20 Just as one and the same all-pervading space exists within and without a jar, so the eternal, everlasting God exists in the totality of things

---

mind and sense is that I have children that get in trouble. Then I have a wife who leaves me. And then I have a bank account that's going down. And I have what's called the virus that is long as I've identified with the objects. So then "I" must suffer. This is the ignorance. You have to burn it down with the knowledge. Intuit that "I am that". I am that absolute pure consciousness, which is the witness of everything. And is uninfected unattached to never bound and ever blissful.

In terms of the example of the mirror and the reflection that superimposed then that reflection on the mirror in relation to the reflection, the mirror, The reflection exists in the mirror, but the mirror is outside the reflection in the same way the whole universe appears in me. But I am outside of the universe.

II *Marvel of the Infinite Self Beyond Nature*

Janaka:

1 Truly I am spotless and at peace, the awareness beyond natural causality. All this time I have been afflicted by delusion.

2 As I alone give light to this body, so I do to the world, As a result the whole world is mine, or alternatively nothing is.

3 So now abandoning the body and everything else, by some good fortune or other my true self becomes apparent.

4 Just as waves, foam and bubbles are not different from water, so all this which has emanated from oneself, is no other than oneself.[6]

---

6 *The waves of the universe of waking and dream arise. They exist in that consciousness, just like the wave can't exist apart from the water. Whatever appears can't appear independent of that. If it abides, it has to abide in that consciousness. And when it ceases, there's*

5 In the same way that cloth is found to be just thread when analysed, so when all this is analysed it is found to be no other than oneself.

6 Just as the sugar produced from the juice of the sugarcane is permeated with the same taste, so all this, produced out of me, is completely permeated with me.

7 From ignorance of oneself, the world appears, and by knowledge of oneself it appears no longer. From ignorance of the rope a snake appears, and by knowledge of it, it appears no longer.

8 Shining is my essential nature, and I am nothing over and beyond that. When the world shines forth, it is simply me that is shining forth.

9 All this appears in me imagined due to ignorance, just as a snake appears in the rope, the mirage of water in the sunlight, and silver in mother of pearl.

---

nowhere else for it to go except to merge into that consciousness.

10 All this, which has originated out of me, is resolved back into me too, like a jug back into clay, a wave into water, and a bracelet into gold.

11 How wonderful I am! Glory be to me, for whom there is no destruction, remaining even beyond the destruction of the world from Brahma down to the last clump of grass.

12 How wonderful I am! Glory be to me, solitary even though with a body, neither going or coming anywhere, I who abide for-ever, filling all that is.

13 How wonderful I am! Glory be to me! There is no one so clever as me! I who have borne all that is forever, without even touch-ing it with my body!

14 How wonderful I am! Glory be to me! I who possess nothing at all, or alternatively possess everything that speech and mind can refer to.

15 Knowledge, what is to be known, and the knower - these three do not exist in real-ity. I am the spotless reality in which they appear because of ignorance.

16 Truly dualism is the root of suffering. There is no other remedy for it than the realization that all this that we see is unreal, and that I am the one stainless reality, consisting of consciousness.

17 I am pure awareness though through ignorance I have imagined myself to have additional attributes. By continually reflecting like this, my dwelling place is in the Unimagined.

18 For me there is neither bondage nor liberation. The illusion has lost its basis and ceased. Truly all this exists in me, though ultimately it does not even exist in me.

19 I have recognized that all this and my body are nothing, While my true self is nothing but pure consciousness, so what can the imagination work on now?

20 The body, heaven and hell, bondage and liberation, and fear too, All this is pure imagination. What is there left to do for me whose very nature is consciousness?

21 Truly I do not see dualism even in a

crowd of people. What pleasure should I have when it has turned into a wilderness?

22 I am not the body, nor is the body mine. I am not a living being. I am consciousness. It was my thirst for living that was my bondage.

23 Truly it is in the limitless ocean of myself, that stimulated by the colourful waves of the worlds everything suddenly arises in the wind of consciousness.

24 It is in the limitless ocean of myself, that the wind of thought subsides, and the trader-like living beings' world bark is wrecked by lack of goods.

25 How wonderful it is that in the limitless ocean of myself the waves of living beings arise, collide, play and disappear, according to their natures.[7]

---

7   *The universe appears in your conscious-ness nowhere else. It can't appear anywhere else. It appears to you. And that universe is like a snake. From the parable of rope and snake; because I don't know.. I mistake the rope as a snake. Oh, is the snake there? The snake appeared to be that snake. However, is not a second thing apart from the rope. There is a*

truth to the snake. The rope is the truth of it. I took it to be a snake, but even when I took it to be a snake, it was still just a rope. And when I realized, Oh, it's only a rope. No snake was destroyed. There never was a snake because it was just superimposed by ignorance. Even though it appeared to exist in truth, it didn't exist. It was appearing due to ignorance. That's the example of the rope and the snake. There's not two things. There's only this Self. Because we're ignorant of the Self. Because I don't know that I'm the witness. I have mistaken myself to be the witnessed. I have superimposed the Universe on myself. The body, mind sense, the ego and the whole universe. It's all superimposed on me the witness. What does that mean? Just like in the snake example. There never really was a universe.

III Self in All and All in the Self

Ashtavakra:

1 Knowing yourself as truly one and indestructible, how could a wise man possessing self-knowledge like you feel any pleasure in acquiring wealth?

2 Truly, when one does not know oneself, one takes pleasure in the objects of mistaken perception, just as greed arises for the mistaken silver in one who does not know mother of pearl for what it is.

3 All this wells up like waves in the sea. Recognizing, "I am That", why run around like someone in need?

4 After hearing of oneself as pure consciousness and the supremely beautiful, is one to go on lusting after sordid sexual objects?

5 When the sage has realized that he himself is in all beings, and all beings are in him, it is astonishing that the sense of individuality should be able to continue.

6 It is astonishing that a man who has reached the supreme non-dual state and is intent on the benefits of liberation should still be subject to lust and held back by sexual activity.

7 It is astonishing that one already very debilitated, and knowing very well that its arousal is the enemy of knowledge should still hanker after sensuality, even when approaching his last days.

8 It is astonishing that one who is unattached to the things of this world or the next, who discriminates between the permanent and the impermanent, and who longs for liberation, should still feel fear for liberation.

9 Whether feted or tormented, the wise man is always aware of his supreme self-nature and is neither pleased nor disappointed.

10 The great souled person sees even his own body in action as if it were some-one else's, so how should he be disturbed by praise or blame?

11 Seeing this world as pure illusion, and devoid of any interest in it, how should the strong-minded person, feel fear, even at the approach of death?

12 Who is to be compared to the great souled person whose mind is free of desire even in disappointment, and who has found satisfaction in self-knowledge?

13 How should a strong-minded person, who knows that what he sees is by its very nature nothing, consider one thing to be grasped and another to be rejected?

14 For someone who has eliminated attachment, and who is free from dualism and from desire, an object of enjoyment that comes of itself is neither painful nor pleasurable.

IV Knower and the Non-knower of the Self

Ashtavakra:

1 Certainly the wise person of self-knowledge, playing the game of worldly enjoyment, bears no resemblance whatever to the world's bewildered beasts of burden.

2 Truly the yogi feels no excitement even at being established in that state which all the Devas from Indra down yearn for disconsolately.

3 He who has known That is untouched within by good deeds or bad, just as the sky is not touched by smoke, however much it may appear to be.

4 Who can prevent the great-souled person who has known this whole world as himself from living as he pleases?

5 Of all four categories of beings, from Brahma down to the last clump of grass, only the man of knowledge is capable of eliminat-

ing desire and aversion.

6 Rare is the man who knows himself[8] as

___

8   *Is called the Spiritual Faculty of the Mind.*
Why? Because when the mind turns inwards,
it's able to recognize the fact that I am the wit-
ness of all phenomena. That's my true nature.
We can intuit that fact with the mind becomes
subtle and pure and introvert like Janika. He
can hear this teaching. And because he's intu-
ited the witness for himself when he hears of
Ashtavakra talking, it's not just words, but he
can verify. I am the witness of all the elements.
I'm not any of the elements. I am unattached.
He can understand that intuitively. Not with
the mind, not with the senses, not with reason-
ing. Because to know that you're the witness
of all reasons, of all senseless. Can't be known
through reasoning or the sense of you have to
intuit the fact of the matter. Add the thoughts,
object or subject. The only way is through
intuition. If you haven't turned inwards. And
see. What is the object and who is the subject?
What is changing and what is not changing?
What is appearing and disappearing. And
what is ever the same. If you're not able to
intuit that, then this teaching is like singing to
the deaf. The words mean nothing, but for a
person, mind is introvert and can intuit that

the undivided Lord of the world, and no fear occurs to him who knows this from anything.

---

when he hears or reads this.

V Stages of Dissolution of Consciousness

Ashtavakra:

1 You are not bound by anything. What does a pure person like you need to renounce? Putting the complex organism to rest, you can go to your rest.

2 All this arises out of you, like a bubble out of the sea. Knowing yourself like this to be but one, you can go to your rest.

3 In spite of being in front of your eyes, all this, being insubstantial, does not exist in you, spotless as you are. It is an appearance like the snake in a rope, so you can go to your rest.

4 Equal in pain and in pleasure, equal in hope and in disappointment, equal in life and in death, and complete as you are, you can go to your rest.

VI Irrelevance of Dissolution of Consciousness

Ashtavakra:

1 I am infinite like space, and the natural world is like a jar. To know this is knowledge, and then there is neither renunciation, acceptance or cessation of it.

2 I am like the ocean[9], and the multiplicity of objects is comparable to a wave. To know this is knowledge, and then there is neither renunciation, acceptance or cessation of it.

3 I am like the mother of pearl, and the

___
9   *The waves, the foams, the bubbles are not different from the water. In this example, if you take the ocean, the ocean is nothing but water out of the ocean. But if I were to take away the ocean, could there be any waves? Could there be any bubbles? Could there be any foam?*

The waves, the bubbles' existence while they are existing is totally dependent upon the ocean. And when they merge. There's nowhere else for them to merge except in the ocean.

imagined world is like the silver. To know this is knowledge, and then there is neither renunciation, acceptance or cessation of it.

4 Alternatively, I am in all beings, and all beings are in me. To know this is knowledge, and then there is neither renunciation, acceptance or cessation of it.

VII Tranquil and Bound-less Ocean of the Self

Janaka:

1 It is in the infinite ocean of myself that the world bark wanders here and there, driven by its own inner wind. I am not upset by that.

2 Let the world wave rise or vanish of its own nature in the infinite ocean of myself. There is no increase or diminution to me from it.

3 It is in the infinite ocean of myself that the imagination called the world takes place. I am supremely peaceful and formless, and as such I remain.

4 My true nature is not contained in objects, nor does any object exist in it, for it is infinite and spotless. So it is unattached, desireless and at peace, and as such I remain.

5 Truly I am but pure consciousness, and the world is like a conjuror's show, so how could I imagine there is anything there to

take up or reject?

VIII Bondage and Freedom

Ashtavakra:

1 Bondage is when the mind longs for something, grieves about something, rejects something, holds on to something, is pleased about something or displeased about something.

2 Liberation is when the mind does not long for anything, grieve about anything, reject anything, or hold on to anything, and is not pleased about anything or displeased about anything.

3 Bondage is when the mind is tangled in one of the senses, and liberation is when the mind is not tangled in any of the senses.

4 When there is no 'me' that is liberation, and when there is 'me' there is bondage. Considering this earnestly, do not hold on and do not reject.[10]

---

10   *When you take that position, the whole waking state in which my body appears, the*

other bodies appear and the whole universe appears. I am the witness not only of this body that appears in the waking state. I am a peer. I'm aware of the whole world that appears in this waking state. The waking state is an object to me. And in that state is the world. And the body mind senses. Is there all object to me? Before I took this to be the subject. I'm the subject and the world is the object. But now I've come to realize even this body, mind, senses and ego is not the subject. It's the object. It appears for a while it gets canceled. During a dream and deep sleep it doesn't appear at all. But I remain the unchanging consciousness in all the states. So not only am I the alumina of this body, I'm the alumina of the whole universe. And because of that, I am one. There's just one light for the whole of duality. Subject and object appear in me.

So now. You've identified, and they're all objects that are coming in, going to you. But you've identified and that is your bondage. This in a that is called ignorance. Even though I'm the witness, and even though this body in the whole universe is the witness I have identified wrongly. And I say, I was born, I'm getting old, I'm getting sick. I'm going to die. That witness, which is never born, which never gets old, which never gets sick, and which never dies

IX Indifference

Ashtavakra:

1 Knowing when the dualism of things done and undone has been put to rest, or the person for whom they occur has, then you can here and now go beyond renunciation and obligations by indifference to such things.

2 Rare indeed, my son, is the lucky man whose observation of the world's behaviour has led to the extinction of his thirst for living, thirst for pleasure and thirst for knowledge.

3 All this is impermanent and spoilt by the three sorts of pain. Recognising it to be insubstantial, comtemptible and only fit for rejection, one attains peace.

---

because of our identification, false identification with the witness. I am bound. It's not a real bandage. You're always the witness, even when you take yourself to be this body. The self remains ever free, but because of the ignorance of that fact, everybody naturally feels I have this. This wrong idea is called bondage.

4 When was that age or time of life when the dualism of extremes did not exist for men? Abandoning them, a person who is happy to take whatever comes attains perfection.

5 Who does not end up with indifference to such things and attain peace when he has seen the differences of opinions among the great sages, saints and yogis?

6 Is he not a guru who, endowed with dispassion[11] and equanimity, achieves full knowledge of the nature of consciousness, and leads others out of Samsara?

---

11 *We have to see them that even though the mind's tendency is to seek happiness outside the one who wants mukti liberation, that mind has to become turned away from them. It'll only turn away from them when it's convinced that the happiness that I'm seeking doesn't reside in the objects.*

In fact, bliss resides in my own true nature, in my own self. That turning away from external objects is called dispassion. There's more to be said about this because it doesn't mean living in a cave.

7 If you would just see the transformations of the elements as nothing more than the elements, then you would immediately be freed from all bonds and established in your own nature.

8 One's inclinations are Samsara. Knowing this, abandon them. The renunciation of them is the renunciation of it. Now you can remain as you are.

X Dispassion

Ashtavakra:

1 Abandoning desire, the enemy, along with gain, itself so full of loss, and the good deeds which are the cause of the other two - practice indifference to everything.

2 Look on such things as friends, land, money, property, wife, and bequests as nothing but a dream or a three or five- day conjuror's show.

3 Wherever a desire occurs, see Samsara in it. Establishing yourself in firm dispassion, be free of passion and happy.

4 The essential nature of bondage is nothing other than desire, and its elimination is known as liberation. It is simply by not being attached to changing things that the everlasting joy of attainment is reached.

5 You are one, conscious and pure, while all this is just inert non-being. Ignorance itself is nothing, so what need have you of desire to understand?

6 Kingdoms, children, wives, bodies, pleasures - these have all been lost to you life after life, attached to them though you were.

7 Enough of wealth, sensuality and good deeds. In the forest of Samsara the mind has never found satisfaction in these.

8 How many births have you not done hard and painful labour with body, mind and speech. Now at last stop!

XI Self as Pure and Radiant Intelligence

Ashtavakra:

1 Unmoved and undistressed, realising that being, non-being and transformation are of the very nature of things, one easily finds peace.

2 At peace, having shed all desires within, and realising that nothing exists here but the Lord, the Creator of all things, one is no longer attached to anything.

3 Realising that misfortune and fortune come in their turn from fate, one is contented, one's senses under control, and does not like or dislike.

4 Realising that pleasure and pain, birth and death are from fate, and that one's desires cannot be achieved, one remains inactive, and even when acting does not get attached.

5 Realising that suffering arises from nothing other than thinking, dropping all desires

one rids oneself of it, and is happy and at peace everywhere.

6 Realising, 'I am not the body, nor is the body mine. I am awareness', one attains the supreme state and no longer remembers things done or undone.

7 Realising, 'It is just me, from Brahma down to the last clump of grass', one becomes free from uncertainty, pure, at peace and unconcerned about what has been attained or not.

8 Realising that all this varied and wonderful world is nothing, one becomes pure receptivity, free from inclinations, and as if nothing existed, one finds peace.

XII Ascent of Contemplation

Janaka:

1 First of all I was averse to physical activity, then to lengthy speech, and finally to thinking itself, which is why I am now established.

2 In the absence of delight in sound and the other senses, and by the fact that I am myself not an object of the senses, my mind is focused and free from distraction - which is why I am now established.

3 Owing to the distraction of such things as wrong identification, one is driven to strive for mental stillness. Recognising this pattern I am now established.

4 By relinquishing the sense of rejection and acceptance, and with pleasure and disappointment ceasing today, Brahmin, I am now established.

5 Life in a community, then going beyond such a state, meditation and the elimination

of mind-made objects - by means of these I have seen my error, and I am now established.

6 Just as the performance of actions is due to ignorance, so their abandonment is too. By fully recognising this truth, I am now established.

7 Trying to think the unthinkable, is doing something unnatural to thought. Abandoning such a practice therefore, I am now established.

8 He who has achieved this has achieved the goal of life. He who is of such a nature has done what has to be done.

XIII Transcendent Bliss

Janaka:

1 The inner freedom of having nothing is hard to achieve, even with just a loin-cloth, but I live as I please abandoning both renunciation and acquisition.

2 Sometimes one experiences distress because of one's body, sometimes because of one's tongue, and sometimes because of one's mind. Abandoning all of these, I live as I please in the goal of human existence.

3 Recognising that in reality no action is ever committed, I live as I please, just doing what presents itself to be done.

4 Yogis who identify themselves with their bodies are insistent on fulfilling and avoiding certain actions, but I live as I please abandoning attachment and rejection.

5 No benefit or loss comes to me by standing, walking or lying down, so consequently I live as I please whether standing, walking or sleeping.

6 I lose nothing by sleeping and gain nothing by effort, so consequently I live as I please,
abandoning loss and success.

7 Frequently observing the drawbacks
of such things as pleasant objects, I live as I
please, abandoning the pleasant and unpleas-
ant.

XIV Natural Dissolution of the Mind

Janaka:

1 He who by nature is empty minded, and who thinks of things only unintentionally, is freed from deliberate remembering like one awakened from a dream.

2 When my desire has been eliminated, I have no wealth, friends, robber senses, scriptures or knowledge?

3 Realising my supreme self-nature in the Person of the Witness, the Lord, and the state of desirelessness in bondage or liberation, I feel no inclination for liberation.

4 The various states of one who is empty of uncertainty within, and who outwardly wanders about as he pleases like a madman, can only be known by someone in the same condition.

XV Unborn Self or Brahman

Ashtavakra:

1 While a man of pure intelligence may achieve the goal by the most casual of instruction, another may seek knowledge all his life and still remain bewildered.

2 Liberation is distaste for the objects of the senses. Bondage is love of the senses. This is knowledge. Now do as you please.

3 This awareness of the truth makes an eloquent, clever and energetic man dumb, stupid and lazy, so it is avoided by those whose aim is enjoyment.

4 You are not the body, nor is the body yours, nor are you the doer of actions or the reaper of their consequences. You are eternally pure consciousness the witness, in need of nothing - so live happily.

5 Desire and anger are objects of the mind, but the mind is not yours, nor ever

has been. You are choiceless, awareness itself and unchanging - so live happily.

6 Recognising oneself in all beings, and all beings in oneself, be happy, free from the sense of responsibility and free from preoccupation with 'me'.

7 Your nature is the consciousness, in which the whole world wells up, like waves in the sea. That is what you are, without any doubt, so be free of disturbance.

8 Have faith, my son, have faith. Don't let yourself be deluded in this, sir. You are yourself the Lord, whose property is knowledge, and are beyond natural causation.

9 The body invested with the senses stands still, and comes and goes. You yourself neither come nor go, so why bother about them?

10 Let the body last to the end of the Age, or let it come to an end right now. What have you gained or lost, who consist of pure consciousness?

11 Let the world wave rise or subside according to its own nature in you, the great

ocean. It is no gain or loss to you.

12 My son, you consist of pure consciousness, and the world is not separate from you. So who is to accept or reject it, and how, and why?

13 How can there be either birth, karma or responsibility in that one unchanging, peaceful, unblemished and infinite consciousness which is you?

14 Whatever you see, it is you alone manifest in it. How could bracelets, armlets and anklets be different from the gold?

15 Giving up such distinctions as 'This is what I am', and 'I am not that', recognise that 'Everything is myself', and be without distinction and happy.

16 It is through your ignorance that all this exists. In reality you alone exist. Apart from you there is no one within or beyond Samsara.

17 Knowing that all this is an illusion, one becomes free from desire, pure receptivity and at peace, as if nothing existed.

18 Only one thing has existed, exists and will exist in the ocean of being. You have no bondage or liberation. Live happily and fulfilled.

19 Being pure consciousness, do not disturb your mind with thoughts[12] of for and against. Be at peace and remain happily in yourself, the essence of joy.

20 Give up the practice of concentration completely and hold nothing in your mind. You are free in your very nature, so what will you achieve by working your brain?

---

12   *Vedanta says the thoughts are not self known. The thoughts appear in consciousness. They abide in consciousness. They are an object of consciousness, and they disappear to consciousness. When the thoughts appear, the thoughts don't know that they appear. Because they appear to who? When the thoughts disappear, they don't know that they disappear because they no longer existed. They disappear. To who? The witness of the thoughts is the true self within.*

XVI Self-Abidance through Obliteration of the World

Ashtavakra:

1 My son, you may recite or listen to count-less scriptures, but you will not be established within until you can forget everything.

2 You may, as a learned man, indulge in wealth, activity and meditation[13], but your mind will still long for that which is the ces-sation of desire, and beyond all goals.

3 It is because of effort that everyone is in pain, but no-one realises it. By just this simple instruction, the lucky one attains tranquility.

---

13   This indeed is your bandage that you practice meditation. This is quite a radical achievement for most people, most yogis say that you have to control your mind and turn in words and stop all the thoughts and stop thinking about. So from the highest point of view. He's able to say to Janika. There's no need for meditation.

4 Happiness belongs to no-one but that supremely lazy man for whom even opening and closing his eyes is a bother.

5 When the mind is freed from such pairs of opposites as, 'I have done this', and 'I have not done that', it becomes indifferent to merit, wealth, sensuality and liberation.

6 One man is abstemious and averse to the senses, another is greedy and attached to them, but he who is free from both taking and rejecting is neither abstemious nor greedy.

7 So long as desire, which is the state of lack of discrimination, remains, the sense of revulsion and attraction will remain, which is the root and branch of Samsara.

8 Desire springs from usage, and aversion from abstention, but the wise man is free from the pairs of opposites like a child, and becomes established.

9 The passionate man wants to be rid of Samsara so as to avoid pain, but the dispassionate man is without pain and feels no distress even in it.

10 He who is proud about even liberation or his own body, and feels them his own, is neither a seer or a yogi. He is still just a sufferer.

11 If even Shiva, Vishnu or the lotus-born Brahma were your instructor, until you have forgotten everything you cannot be established within.

XVII Absolute Aloneness of the Self

Ashtavakta said:

1 He who is content, with purified senses, and always enjoys solitude, has gained the fruit of knowledge and the fruit of the practice of yoga too.

2 The knower of truth is never distressed in this world, for the whole round world is full of himself alone.

3 None of these senses please a man who has found satisfaction within, just as Nimba leaves do not please the elephant that has a taste for Sallaki leaves.

4 Not attached to the things he has enjoyed, and not hankering after the things he has not enjoyed, such a man is hard to find.

5 Those who desire pleasure and those who desire liberation are both found in Samsara, but the great souled man who desires neither pleasure nor liberation is rare indeed.

6 It is only the noble minded who is free from attraction or repulsion to religion, wealth, sensuality, and life and death too.

7 He feels no desire for the elimination of all this, nor anger at its continuing, so the lucky man lives happily with whatever means of sustenance presents itself.

8 Thus fulfilled through this knowledge, contented and with the thinking mind emptied, he lives happily just seeing, hearing, feeling, smelling and tasting.

9 In him for whom the ocean of Samsara has dried up, there is neither attachment or aversion. His gaze is vacant, his behaviour purposeless, and his senses inactive.

10 Surely the supreme state is everywhere for the liberated mind. He is neither awake or asleep, and neither opens or closes his eyes.
11 The liberated man is resplendent everywhere, free from all desires. Everywhere he appears self-possessed and pure of heart.

12 Seeing, hearing, feeling, smelling, tasting, speaking and walking about, the great

souled man who is freed from trying to achieve or avoid anything is free indeed.

13 The liberated man is free from desires everywhere. He does not blame, does not praise, does not rejoice, is not disappointed, and neither gives nor takes.

14 When a great souled one is equally unperturbed in mind and self-possessed at the sight of a woman full of desire and at approaching death, he is truly liberated.

15 There is no distinction between pleasure and pain, man and woman, success and failure for the wise man who looks on everything as equal.

16 There is no aggression or compassion, no pride or humility, no wonder or confusion for the man whose days of running about are over.

17 The liberated man is not averse to the senses and nor is he attached to them. He enjoys himself continually with an unattached mind in both achievement and non-achievement.

18 One established in the Absolute state with an empty mind does not know the alternatives of inner stillness and lack of stillness, and of good and evil.

19 Free of 'me' and 'mine' and of a sense of responsibility, aware that 'Nothing exists', with all desires extinguished within, a man does not act even in acting.

20 He whose thinking mind is dissolved achieves the indescribable state and is free from the mental display of delusion, dream and ignorance.

XVIII Way and Goal of Natural Samadhi

Ashtavakra:

1 Praise be to that by the awareness of which delusion itself becomes dream-like, to that which is pure happiness, peace and light.

2 One may get all sorts of pleasure by the acquisition of various objects of enjoyment, but one cannot be happy except by the renunciation of everything.

3 How can there be happiness, for one who is burnt inside by the blistering sun of the pain of things that need doing, without the rain of the nectar of peace?

4 This existence is just imagination. It is nothing in reality, but there is no non-being for natures that know how to distinguish being from non being.

5 The realm of one's own self is not far away, and nor can it be achieved by the addition of limitations to its nature. It is unimagi-

nable, effortless, unchanging and spotless.

6 By the simple elimination of delusion and the recognition of one's true nature, those whose vision is unclouded live free from sorrow.

7 Knowing everything as just imagination, and himself as eternally free, how should the wise man behave like a fool?

8 Knowing himself to be God and being and non-being just imagination, what should the man free from desire learn, say or do?

9 Considerations like 'I am this' or 'I am not this' are finished for the yogi who has gone silent realising 'Everything is myself'.

10 For the yogi who has found peace, there is no distraction or one-pointedness, no higher knowledge or ignorance, no pleasure and no pain.

11 The dominion of heaven or beggary, gain or loss, life among men or in the forest, these make no difference to a yogi whose nature it is to be free from distinctions.

12 There is no religion, wealth, sensuality or discrimination for a yogi free from the pairs of opposites such as 'I have done this' and 'I have not done that'.

13 There is nothing needing to be done, or any attachment in his heart for the yogi liberated while still alive. Things are just for a life-time.

14 There is no delusion, world, meditation on That, or liberation for the pacified great soul. All these things are just the realm of imagination.

15 He by whom all this is seen may well make out he doesn't exist, but what is the desireless one to do? Even in seeing he does not see.

16 He by whom the Supreme Brahma is seen may think 'I am Brahma', but what is he to think who is without thought, and who sees no duality.

17 He by whom inner distraction is seen may put an end to it, but the noble one is not distracted. When there is nothing to achieve, what is he to do?

18 The wise man, unlike the worldly man, does not see inner stillness, distraction or fault in himself, even when living like a worldly man.

19 Nothing is done by him who is free from being and non- being, who is contented, desireless and wise, even if in the world's eyes he does act.

20 The wise man who just goes on doing what presents itself for him to do, encounters no difficulty in either activity or inactivity.

21 He who is desireless, self-reliant, independent and free of bonds functions like a dead leaf blown about by the wind of causality.

22 There is neither joy nor sorrow for one who has transcended Samsara. He lives always with a peaceful mind and as if without a body.

23 He whose joy is in himself, and who is peaceful and pure within has no desire for renunciation or sense of loss in anything.

24 For the man with a naturally empty mind, doing just as he pleases, there is no such thing as pride or false humility, as there is for the natural man.

25 'This action was done by the body but not by me'. The pure- natured person thinking like this, is not acting even when acting.

26 He who acts without being able to say why, but not because he is a fool, he is one liberated while still alive, happy and blessed. He thrives even in Samsara.

27 He who has had enough of endless considerations and has attained to peace, does not think, know, hear or see.

28 He who is beyond mental stillness and distraction, does not desire either liberation or anything else. Recognising that things are just constructions of the imagination, that great soul lives as God here and now.

29 He who feels responsibility within, acts even when not acting, but there is no sense of done or undone for the wise man who is free from the sense of responsibility.

30 The mind of the liberated man is not upset or pleased. It shines unmoving, desireless, and free from doubt.

31 He whose mind does not set out to meditate or act, meditates and acts without an object.

32 A stupid man is bewildered when he hears the real truth, while even a clever man is humbled by it just like the fool.

33 The ignorant make a great effort to practise one-pointedness and the stopping of thought, while the wise see nothing to be done and remain in themselves like those asleep.

34 The stupid does not attain cessation whether he acts or abandons action, while the wise man find peace within simply by knowing the truth.

35 People cannot come to know themselves by practices - pure awareness, clear, complete, beyond multiplicity and faultless though they are.

36 The stupid does not achieve liberation

even through regular practice, but the fortunate remains free and actionless simply by discrimination.

37 The stupid does not attain Godhead because he wants to become it, while the wise man enjoys the Supreme Godhead without even wanting it.

38 Even when living without any support and eager for achievement, the stupid are still nourishing Samsara, while the wise have cut at the very root of its unhappiness.

39 The stupid does not find peace because he is wanting it, while the wise discriminating the truth is always peaceful minded.

40 How can there be self knowledge for him whose knowledge depends on what he sees. The wise do not see this and that, but see themselves as unending.

41 How can there be cessation of thought for the misguided who is striving for it. Yet it is there always naturally for the wise man delighted in himself.

42 Some think that something exists, and

others that nothing does. Rare is the man who does not think either, and is thereby free from distraction.

43 Those of weak intelligence think of themselves as pure nonduality, but because of their delusion do not know this, and remain unfulfilled all their lives.

44 The mind of the man seeking liberation can find no resting place within, but the mind of the liberated man is always free from desire by the very fact of being without a resting place.

45 Seeing the tigers of the senses, the frightened refuge- seekers at once enter the cave in search of cessation of thought and one-pointedness.

46 Seeing the desireless lion the elephants of the senses silently run away, or, if they cannot, serve him like courtiers.

47 The man who is free from doubts and whose mind is free does not bother about means of liberation. Whether seeing, hearing, feeling smelling or tasting, he lives at ease.

48 He whose mind is pure and undistracted from the simple hearing of the Truth sees neither something to do nor something to avoid nor a cause for indifference.

49 The straightforward person does whatever arrives to be done, good or bad, for his actions are like those of a child.

50 By inner freedom one attains happiness, by inner freedom one reaches the Supreme, by inner freedom one comes to absence of thought, by inner freedom to the Ultimate State.

51 When one sees oneself as neither the doer nor the reaper of the consequences, then all mind waves come to an end.

52 The spontaneous unassumed behaviour of the wise is noteworthy, but not the deliberate, intentional stillness of the fool.

53 The wise who are rid of imagination, unbound and with unfettered awareness may enjoy themselves in the midst of many goods, or alternatively go off to mountain caves.

54 There is no attachment in the heart of a wise man whether he sees or pays homage to a learned Brahmin, a celestial being, a holy place, a woman, a king or a friend.

55 A yogi is not in the least put out even when humiliated by the ridicule of servants, sons, wives, grandchildren or other relatives.

56 Even when pleased he is not pleased, not suffering even when in pain. Only those like him can know the wonderful state of such a man.

57 It is the sense of responsibility which is Samsara. The wise who are of the form of emptiness, formless, unchanging and spotless see no such thing.

58 Even when doing nothing the fool is agitated by restlessness, while a skilful man remains undisturbed even when doing what there is to do.

59 Happy he stands, happy he sits, happy sleeps and happy he comes and goes. Happy he speaks, and happy he eats. Such is the life of a man at peace.

60 He who of his very nature feels no unhappiness in his daily life like worldly people, remains undisturbed like a great lake, all sorrow gone.

61 Even abstention from action leads to action in a fool, while even the action of the wise man brings the fruits of inaction.

62 A fool often shows aversion towards his belongings, but for him whose attachment to the body has dropped away, there is neither attachment nor aversion.

63 The mind of the fool is always caught in an opinion about becoming or avoiding something, but the wise man's nature is to have no opinions about becoming and avoiding.

64 For the seer who behaves like a child, without desire in all actions, there is no attachment for such a pure one even in the work he does.

65 Blessed is he who knows himself and is the same in all states, with a mind free from craving whether he is seeing, hearing, feeling, smelling or tasting.

66 There is no man subject to Samsara, sense of individuality, goal or means to the goal for the wise man who is always free from imaginations, and unchanging as space.

67 Glorious is he who has abandoned all goals and is the incarnation of satisfaction, his very nature, and whose inner focus on the Unconditioned is quite spontaneous.

68 In brief, the great-souled man who has come to know the Truth is without desire for either pleasure or liberation, and is always and everywhere free from attachment.

69 What remains to be done by the man who is pure awareness and has abandoned everything that can be expressed in words from the highest heaven to the earth itself?

70 The pure man who has experienced the Indescribable attains peace by his own nature, realising that all this is nothing but illusion, and that nothing is.

71 There are no rules, dispassion, renunciation or meditation for one who is pure receptivity by nature, and admits no know-

able form of being?

72 For him who shines with the radiance of Infinity and is not subject to natural causality there is neither bondage, liberation, pleasure nor pain.

73 Pure illusion reigns in Samsara which will continue until self realisation, but the enlightened man lives in the beauty of freedom from me and mine, from the sense of responsibility and from any attachment.

74 For the seer who knows himself as imperishable and beyond pain there is neither knowledge, a world nor the sense that I am the body or the body mine.

75 No sooner does a man of low intelligence give up activities like the elimination of thought than he falls into mental chariot racing and babble.

76 A fool does not get rid of his stupidity even on hearing the truth. He may appear outwardly free from imaginations, but inside he is hankering after the senses still.

77 Though in the eyes of the world he is

active, the man who has shed action through knowledge finds no means of doing or speaking anything.

78 For the wise man who is always unchanging and fearless there is neither darkness nor light nor destruction, nor anything.

79 There is neither fortitude, prudence nor courage for the yogi whose nature is beyond description and free of individuality.

80 There is neither heaven nor hell nor even liberation during life. In a nutshell, in the sight of the seer nothing exists at all.

81 He neither longs for possessions nor grieves at their absence. The calm mind of the sage is full of the nectar of immortality.

82 The dispassionate does not praise the good or blame the wicked. Content and equal in pain and pleasure, he sees nothing that needs doing.

83 The wise man does not dislike Samsara or seek to know himself. Free from pleasure and impatience, he is not dead and he is not alive.

84 The wise man stands out by being free from anticipation, without attachment to such things as children or wives, free from desire for the senses, and not even concerned about his own body.

85 Peace is everywhere for the wise man who lives on whatever happens to come to him, going to wherever he feels like, and sleeping wherever the sun happens to set.

86 Let his body rise or fall. The great souled one gives it no thought, having forgotten all about Samsara in coming to rest on the ground of his true nature.

87 The wise man has the joy of being complete in himself and without possessions, acting as he pleases, free from duality and rid of doubts, and without attachment to any creature.

88 The wise man excels in being without the sense of 'me'. Earth, a stone or gold are the same to him. The knots of his heart have been rent asunder, and he is freed from greed and blindness.

89 Who can compare with that contented, liberated soul who pays no regard to anything and has no desire left in his heart?

90 Who but the upright man without desire knows without knowing, sees without seeing and speaks without speaking?

91 Beggar or king, he excels who is without desire, and whose opinion of things is rid of 'good' and 'bad'.

92 There is neither dissolute behaviour nor virtue, nor even discrimination of the truth for the sage who has reached the goal and is the very embodiment of guileless sincerity.

93 How can one describe what is experienced within by one desireless and free from pain, and content to rest in himself - and of whom?

94 The wise man who is contented in all circumstances is not asleep even in deep sleep, not sleeping in a dream, nor waking when he is awake.

95 The seer is without thoughts even when thinking, without senses among the senses,

without understanding even in understanding and without a sense of responsibility even in the ego.

96 Neither happy nor unhappy, neither detached nor attached, neither seeking liberation nor liberated, he is neither something nor nothing.

97 Not distracted in distraction, in mental stillness not poised, in stupidity not stupid, that blessed one is not even wise in his wisdom.

98 The liberated man is self-possessed in all circumstances and free from the idea of 'done' and 'still to do'. He is the same wherever he is and without greed. He does not dwell on what he has done or not done.

99 He is not pleased when praised nor upset when blamed. He is not afraid of death nor attached to life.

100 A man at peace does not run off to popular resorts or to the forest. Whatever and wherever, he remains the same.

XIX Majesty of the Self

Janaka:

1 Using the tweezers of the knowledge of the truth I have managed to extract the painful thorn of endless opinions from the recesses of my heart.

2 For me, established in my own glory, there is no religion, sensuality, possessions, philosophy, duality or even non- duality.

3 For me established in my own glory, there is no past, future or present. There is no space or even eternity.

4 For me established in my own glory, there is no self or non- self, no good or evil, no thought or even absence of thought.

5 For me established in my own glory, there is no dreaming or deep sleep, no waking nor fourth state beyond them, and certainly no fear.

6 For me established in my own glory,

there is nothing far away and nothing near, nothing within or without, nothing large and nothing small.

7 For me established in my own glory, there is no life or death, no worlds or things of the world, no distraction and no stillness of mind.

8 For me remaining in myself, there is no need for talk of the three goals of life, of yoga or of knowledge.

XX *Transcendence of the Self*

Janaka:

1 In my unblemished nature there are no elements, no body, no faculties, no mind. There is no void and no anguish.

2 For me, free from the sense of dualism, there are no scriptures, no self-knowledge, no mind free from an object, no satisfaction and no freedom from desire.

3 There is no knowledge or ignorance, no 'me', 'this' or 'mine', no bondage, no liberation and no property of self-nature.

4 For him who is always free from individual characteristics there is no antecedent causal action, no liberation during life, and no fulfilment at death.

5 For me free from individuality, there is no doer and no reaper of the consequences, no cessation of action, no arising of thought, no immediate object, and no idea of results.

6 There is no world, no seeker for liberation, no yogi, no seer, no-one bound and no-one liberated. I remain in my own non-dual nature.

7 There is no emanation or return, no goal, means, seeker or achievement. I remain in my own non-dual nature.

8 For I am forever unblemished; there is no judge, no standard, nothing to judge, and no judgement.

9 For I am forever actionless; there is no distraction or one-pointedness of mind, no lack of understanding, no stupidity, no joy and no sorrow.

10 For I am always free from deliberations; there is neither conventional truth nor absolute truth, no happiness and no suffering.

11 For I am forever pure; there is no illusion, no Samsara, no attachment or detachment, no living being and no God.

12 For I am forever immovable and indivisible, established in myself; there is no

activity or inactivity, no liberation and no bondage.

13 For I am blessed and without limitation; there is no initiation or scripture, no disciple or teacher and no goal of human existence.

14 There is no being or non-being, no unity or dualism. What more is there to say?

15 Nothing arises out of me.[14]

---

14   *The Self doesn't know anything. If it knew anything, duality would be real.*
But the highest truth is there is no creation. There is no destruction. There is nobody bound. There's nobody practicing spiritual discipline. There's nobody who desires liberation. And there's nobody liberated.

Translator's Notes

There is little doubt though that it is very old, probably dating back to the days of the classic Vedanta period. The Sanskrit style and the doctrine expressed would seem to warrant this assessment.

The work was known, appreciated and quoted by Ramakrishna and his disciple Vivekananda, as well as by Ramana Maharshi, while Radhakrishnan always refers to it with great respect. Apart from that the work speaks for itself. It presents the traditional teachings of Vedanta with a clarity and power very rarely matched.

The translation here is by John Richards, and is presented to the public domain with his affection. The work has been constant inspiration in his life for many years. May it be so for many others.

John   Richards, Stackpole Elidor,   UK (jhr@elidor.demon.co.uk) Presented to the public domain
.94 -- HTML by Gene R. Thursby   .98